"Scott has an amazing ability to take sacred and connect them with a spiritual message."

- Ron Johnson, Senior Pastor, One Church

"Scott and his team are creative and innovative bombs for world evangelism and the finishing of the great commission of our Lord Jesus Christ! Evoke carries an apostolic revolutionary message to empower and prepare the body of Christ to reach an urban young generation in these last minutes of what the Bible calls the end time harvest."

- Johannes Amritzer, President and Founder, Mission SOS international.

"Scott is exceptionally creative and artistic. His heart is burning to see this generation won for Jesus Christ. I see God's hand on him and recommend him highly."

- Reinhard Bonnke, Founder, Christ for all Nations

"I have yet to meet another as vastly creative and simultaneously filled with God. Scott Howe has penned a masterpiece for the creative Christian. The Spirit of the Lord has come upon Him to inspire your creativity to be nothing short of an expression of God Himself."

- Eric Gilmour, Founder, Sonship International

kingdom creativity

understanding the creative ways of God and your unique place in His Kingdom

scott howe

Images in the book:

"DNA" graphic design by Scott Howe, pg 17
"Wooden blocks" photo by Scott Howe, pg 24
"Imagine" graphic design by Scott Howe, pg 31
"Keys" photo by Scott Howe, pg 41
"Sword of the Spirit" Acrylic painting by Revel Artist, pg 52
"Red Blue Cross" graphic design by JR Avila, pg 60
"Creative Military" graphic design by Scott Howe, pg 67
"Mountains Sketchbook" graphic design by Scott Howe, pg 76
"Casa Ester" photo by Michael Harrison, graphic design by Scott Howe, pg 82
"Golden Cross" graphic design by JR Avila, pg 92
"Hear God" graphic design by Scott Howe, pg 98
"Lion" Acrylic Painting by Revel Artist, pg 105
"Buildings Abstract" by JR Avila, pg 113

CONTENTS

INTRO

nderstanding the creative aspect of God's personality can help us in every area of our lives. It will help you to discern Him in everyday life, to hear His voice in your prayer time, to see Him speaking all around you, and it will help you to partner with Him as you co-labor together. It will also help you to be more effective in your call, career, relationships, and in virtually every aspect of your life. It will cause you to walk in greater creativity.

When we talk about kingdom creativity, I think most of us approach this topic understanding at least one main thing; we would all say that God is creative. In fact, we read in scripture, "In the beginning, God created the heavens and the earth." (Gen 1:1) In the beginning, we are introduced to God as the creator. As we continue reading the book of Genesis the magnificent creative acts of God continues as he forms and fashions planet earth, and it is absolutely breathtaking.

But understanding God as the creator of heaven and earth is only one part of the revelation here. Sure, it's a HUGE part. But, God is not only a creator, his NATURE is creative. Throughout Scripture, we see that God is solving problems, communicating with his people, revealing Himself, and accomplishing His will and agenda in all types of creative ways. So it's not only that God creates, but His very nature and character ARE peculiar and out of the ordinary, we might say out of this world or "otherly". This reveals to us some-

God is not only a creator but His NATURE is creative

thing very fundamental about His personality and make up.

For example: Just as the act of healing reveals Jesus as compassionate and caring, the act of creating reveals God's creative personality.

One of the dictionary definitions for CREATIVITY goes something like this:

CREATIVITY: The ability to transcend traditional ideas, rules, patterns, relationships, and create meaningful new ideas, forms, methods, and interpretations. This sounds a lot like, "My ways are higher than your ways, my thoughts are higher than your thoughts". (Isaiah 55)

As we tackle this subject of kingdom creativity, we are digging deeper into the characteristics and nature of God in order to draw closer to him and more clearly understand his ways. For those who are artists, technicians or creatives, you will more clearly understand yourself, your talents, your call and your creative relationship to the Lord, for God himself is a creative.

PART 1

UNIQUE GOD

God is huge! Just look at the universe and all the space we have. Science estimates there are over a billion trillion stars, and 10 billion galaxies. There are millions of species of plants and animals. In fact, more than 10,000 new species are discovered every year! Amazing! There is no doubt that the Lord is a prolific creator. Thanks to Edwin Hubble, astronomers estimate that the universe continues to expand at approximately 68km/s per mega parsec... I'm not exactly sure what that means but it's awesome!

Consider this scripture: "For by him all things were created, in heaven and on earth, visible and invisible, whether thrones or dominions or rulers or authorities—all things were created through him and for him." (Colossians 1:16) Side note: if you haven't seen the video by Louie Giglio called "How Great is our God," you should definitely watch it. It's mind-boggling.

There is no doubt that God is a prolific creator; he does that very well, but WHO & WHAT HE IS is also unusually unique. What I mean is that his very makeup and his nature scrambles our brains. Honestly in my former days of atheism the Christian God sounded right out of a fairy tale. A God who is everywhere all the time and can hear every single prayer, and he cares! That's wild. A God who you cannot see or hear who became a man born from a virgin to save us from sin and will return to the earth

God knows no boundaries. He is without measure

- strange! A God who orders around angelic creatures, combatting a sinister team of fallen angels - it all sounds so crazy.

No doubt that the things of the Lord are really OUT OF THIS WORLD! It can become easy after some time to get too familiar with the Lord and make him somehow more like us than he really is.

Consider some of these attributes of our God:

Our God is Infinite: God knows no boundaries. He is without measure.

Our God is Sovereign: He rules his entire creation. He is all knowing and all-powerful.

Our God Always Existed: When Moses asked who he was talking to in the burning bush, God said, "I AM THE ONE WHO ALWAYS IS." God has no beginning or end. He just exists. Nothing else in all the universe is self-caused...only God.

Our God is Wise. Romans 11:33: "Oh, how great are God's riches and wisdom and knowledge! How impossible it is for us to understand his decisions and his ways!"

Our God is Holy: There is absolutely no sin or evil thought in God at all. God is light, God is love. In him there is no darkness. All his ways are right and just.

What he has said in the Bible about himself is true.

Our God is Faithful: Everything that God has promised will come to pass. His faithfulness guarantees this fact. He does not lie. What he has said in the Bible about himself is true. Jesus even said that 'he is' the Truth.

Our God, to accomplish his will, sent the Son by the Spirit to be the incarnation of the Holy One on the earth. Jesus Christ, as the incarnation of the divine, lived in the divine, mystical realm here on earth, becoming the reality of true reconciliation between God and man in essence and in nature. Colossians 1:15 states that, *"The Son is the image of the invisible God"*.

Our God is one yet triune: He said, "Let us make man in our image, according to our likeness." (Gen 1:26-27) God created man in his own image. Our God is one yet in three persons, the Father, the Son & Holy Spirit and all are all CALLED God, are WORSHIPPED as God, and are involved in the workings of God. Although, God reveals himself in three persons, God is One and cannot be divided. All are involved completely, whenever One of the Three is active.

Our God is absolutely unique and very creative in ALL that he IS! Some of these things are beyond our understanding but they remain such a beautiful description of who God is.

Let's never, ever, ever forget how amazing, how majestic, how beyond us is our living God. He is incredible. We are interacting with an amazing indescribable being and he is your heavenly father. If you want further WOW factor read Job 38 and Psalm 104.

God Speaks Uniquely

Not only is God, himself, indescribably unique, but, because it's his nature, he also communicates very creatively, even oddly, we might say. And he doesn't speak to his people all the same way or in the same method. He interacts very differently with each of us. One thing for sure, if we are only listening for the Lord to speak in our conventional methods we will certainly miss much of what he has to reveal.

God spoke to Moses through a bush on fire. (Exodus 3) As Moses took note of the bush on fire, he saw that it wasn't burning into ashes. So Moses came near to the bush and that's when he encountered God...and then the Lord began to speak to him. You see, it wasn't until Moses took notice, or turned aside to see the sign, that he encountered the Lord. How many of us miss the strange or odd signs, that the Lord is calling to us through, to try to get our attention?

God spoke to Saul, who became the apostle Paul, even more dramatically. (Acts 9) Saul was on his way to another city to beat down and arrest

Christians in the name of God, and the Lord showed up in the middle of the road as a bright light. There's no way Saul could've missed God on that one, but it does show us that the Lord will do what he's got to do to get our attention sometimes. He is SEEKING and SAVING. In fact, my salvation experience is somewhat similar.

My Salvation story includes a cast of strange characters including a club DJ, a Frito Lay chip delivery man, a non-practicing Catholic, a real old Jehovah's Witness lady, an ex drug dealer, TV Evangelist, and a bunch of bold believers strategically placed at the right time. I won't get into all the details, but I will tell you this: I was an

He is SEEKING and SAVING.

atheist and never had encountered God in anyway. One night in my apartment, with my girlfriend, through a series of circumstances, the Lord showed up. My girlfriend fell to the ground under the presence of God while I looked on... confused. And when she stood to her feet and began to share the gospel of Jesus Christ with me, I also, for the first time, felt the loving embrace and sweet presence of God; His heart of love, his arms of safety and his wonderful peace.

Balaam is a bizarre story. (Numbers 22) Balaam inquired of the Lord a 2ⁿᵈ time for an answer, after the Lord had already told him what to do. Then he went and disobeyed. As he rode along on his donkey in disobedience, the Angel of the Lord showed up in the middle of the road with a sword! Balaam didn't see him but the donkey did. God in his mercy opened the donkey's mouth and he spoke to Balaam to warn him! An animal speaking!?! Then Balaam's eyes were opened to see. We have to learn to rec-

The Lord will sometimes even speak through children or unbelievers, animals and nature.

ognize the unlikely characters that God uses to lead us in our decisions. That's why we need Godly community. But the Lord will sometimes even speak through children or unbelievers, animals and nature. We need to be listening.

The Lord still shows up today in wonderful ways, drawing people to himself, that their soul may be saved and come into this amazing experience into the kingdom of God.

So what do all these things reveal? They reveal that God is unique in how he speaks to his people. Many people who are sceptics say to me on the streets, "If God begins speaking to me, then

MAYBE I would start to believe". They fail to realize that all around them the Lord is revealing himself, calling out to them. As we read the accounts in scripture and hear the unique testimonies of people who have come into Christ, we see how very different and many times abstract their experiences were. These encounters are not revealing a PATTERN of burning bushes, talking donkeys or bright lights. We often want to reduce the scripture to principals and miss the point. The point is this: God is speaking to individuals, uniquely, the way that he sees fit in apparently random ways and situations. We need to be aware, with hearts wide open, ready to see and hear his "voice" and "leading" in every scenario. As we do, we begin to more clearly hear and follow his will for our lives. It also enables you to encourage and point out the dealings of God in the lives of those around you.

God is speaking to individuals, uniquely, in apparently random ways and situations.

God's solutions are unique

Throughout Scripture we see these real interesting situations that God's people get into and we get to witness how God responds and leads them in very unusual, supernatural ways to bring about a good outcome. The Lord is for his people. Whether we are praying for a healing, fighting a battle, need finances or provision, strength, clarity, or wisdom, God is showing up with all kinds of solutions. We can trust him. But he doesn't always answer the way we think or want.

Sickness & Healing

God performs healings of all kinds, in so many different ways; there doesn't seem to be a pattern. Jesus anointed a blind man's eyes with mud made from his spit, (John 9:6), Elisha had commander Naaman go to the river and wash 7 times. His

leprosy was healed. (2 Kings 5) God had Moses make a bronze sculpture of a snake so that those bitten would be healed. (Numbers 21) Sometimes Jesus simply declared a word. (Luke 18:42)

I spoke with a young homeless man who was waiting in line under a bridge, at night, to get a bowl of soup. He asked for prayer because he had a painful stomach ulcer. When he told me he was an addict, my heart became overwhelmed with the Father's heart and I began to share God's deep love for him. I held him and we both began to cry, when suddenly

God had Moses make a bronze sculpture of a snake so that those bitten would be healed.

he pushed me away. With great joy he explained that he felt an energy all over his body and the pain of his stomach ulcer was gone. I didn't even get a chance to pray for his stomach! I never got past telling him of the love of God before the Lord healed him. Jesus is so wonderful!

In a city-wide meeting called "Winning Your City", I had set up stacks of wooden blocks in the shape of the city skyline. At the altar call I motioned for everyone to come forward and grab a block which represented their role in building the kingdom of God in their city. A young woman, a teacher, who

was involved with street outreaches to children, was suffering from severe pain in her arm. She was getting concerned that if the pain kept increasing she may not be able to continue doing her ministry for the Lord. She came forward for prayer. As she reached out her hand and took a hold of one of those blocks, God's healing power shot right through her arm and the pain vanished. Wow! She gave testimony the next morning in her church on how God had healed her and blessed her to continue her work.

I stood on a platform in Africa as pastors cut chains off of a psychotic madman who had just came to his right mind after the gospel was preached. I saw three little blind sisters, brought to our meeting by their hopeful mama, instantly receive their sight! All three! Our God is a good, good Father!

We can be confident that it is the Lord's will to heal the sick, because Jesus atoned for it on the cross, but the way in which he will bring the healing remains as unique as his character. When praying for someone to be healed or believing for healing yourself, consider the ways of God and listen for his guidance.

Winning Fights

Our God is mighty in battle. That's good to know because we are often in a battle for something! Our lives are full of fights. It might seem you are always struggling with something, but the Lord shows his strength on your behalf as you push on, trusting him and his word.

In Joshua 10 we see a great battle going on. A group of kings joined forces and armies to attack Joshua and his men. But, Joshua had a word from the Lord not to fear, but to be courageous because they would win the battle. As they pressed forward the war was being won by Israel, but the sun began to set. Joshua prayed to the Lord that the sun would not go down until the battle had been won. The Scripture says that the sun stopped in the midst of heaven and did not hurry to set for about a whole day, and there has been no day like it before or since. Joshua prayed and stopped the sun!?! What an amazing story! That is who our God is! What a bizarre way to win a war! This kind of stuff is real! I wonder how many of us have enough faith to pray that kind of prayer? Joshua definitely knew his God, his ways and his abilities. When we begin to know Jesus in a closer way, we pray things according to who HE IS and not just according to our needs. The Holy Spirit has a way about him.

Most of us have heard the story of Joshua and Jericho. (Joshua 6) The Lord showed up and laid out this outrageous war plan to defeat and take over the city of Jericho. *"You shall march around the city, all the men of war going around the city once. Thus shall you do for six days. Seven priests shall bear seven trumpets of rams' horns before the ark. On the seventh day you shall march around the city seven times, and the priests shall blow the trumpets. And when they make a long blast with the ram's horn, when you hear the sound of the trumpet, then all the people shall shout with a great shout, and the wall of the city will fall down flat."* Wow, that plan would certainly not fly at the Pentagon in Washington DC while discussing war strategies, but that was God's plan!

Joshua prayed and stopped the sun!?!

King Jehoshaphat had a great multitude coming against him. (2 Chronicles 20) Scripture tells us he was afraid and set his face to seek the Lord and fast. God assured him that they would not even have to fight, and the Lord would deliver them.

As the army pressed in, King Jehoshaphat sent out the worship team in front of his army. They were singing and praising the Lord, dressed in holy attire. As they sang, <u>the Lord set an ambush</u> against their enemy and they never had to swing a sword! God's ways are not our ways!

You see God may not fight the way we would like to fight, but he always has the victory in mind. Consider every situation you're battling. Ask the Lord and then listen, and he will show you the strategy needed to overcome in your situation. Be open to move in obedience, whatever the Lord calls you to do. Even if it makes little sense.

Amazing occurrences

In Genesis 30 we read about Jacob and his unfortunate events with his uncle, Laban. Laban was a deceitful guy and cheated Jacob regarding marriage arrangements with his daughters. But the Lord blessed Jacob with a strange financial strategy. In those days, spotted and speckled lambs were not as valuable as spotless lambs. As Jacob pastured Laban's flock, his wages were to be the new born, less valuable, striped, spotted & speckled lambs. The Lord gave him wisdom to breed the sheep in front of striped and spotted trees which produced striped and spotted offspring. I don't know that this is scientific, but the Lord gave him favor and wisdom. Soon he had more lambs than he could handle and had to move his entire family. Our heavenly father provides in many outrageous ways!

We read about Elisha, in 2 Kings 6. As he is swinging his axe, the axe head flies off into the river. He is stressed because he borrowed it. Elijah comes over, floats a stick on the water in the area that it sunk and makes the iron axe head float!

Shadrach, Meshach, and Abednego are thrown into the super hot flames meant to incinerate them, but they just stood in the fire. In fact Jesus shows up with them IN the fire. They stood against the king in faith and were not burned. (Daniel 3:8-30)

Philip is lead by the Holy Spirit to share the gospel of Jesus Christ with an Ethiopian Eunuch riding along in his horse and carriage.

Sidenote, the Lord doesn't even stop the carriage. Philip has to run along aside it and strike up a conversation. So he shows up on the scene, jumps into a moving carriage, shares the gospel, baptizes the eunuch and then disappears! The scripture says he was transported or translated away and appeared somewhere else. (Acts 8:26-40)

Elijah rides away into glory on a fiery chariot. (II Kings 2:11) Enoch never died, but was just taken away. (Gen. 5:24) There are testimonies of the old mystics levitating while preaching, taming **Enoch never died, but was just taken away.** wild animals, even appearing in multiple places at one time. Ministries around the world today have reported metal rods in people's back and legs totally dissolving as the person is healed.

These are wild stories, but totally consistent with our God. What is too great for him? *Our God is able to do immeasurably more than all we ask or imagine, according to his power that is at work within us, to him be glory in the church and in Christ Jesus throughout all generations, forever and ever! Amen. Ephesians 3:19-21*

more than you
can ask or
imagine

What limits have you put on God in your life? - Limiting him in what he will do AND how he will do it?

The disciples walked with Jesus. They saw him heal the sick and they saw him cast out many devils. They knew he had authority and moved in the supernatural. Yet, in Mark 4, as they crossed the raging sea through a great windstorm, Jesus woke up and **God is not going to change** rebuked the wind and said to the sea, "Peace be still!" The disciple's response is amazing. *"Who is this, that even the wind and the sea obey him?"* Somehow this event shocked them. It took them deeper into the revelation of Jesus than they had ever been before. Whether you know it or not, you have put limitations on what God really CAN do and CANNOT do, or what he WILL do and what he WILL NOT do.

God is not going to change. He invites us into his world, into his realm to co-labor, co-create and partner with him on his terms. The more you get to know his ways, the more you will recognize his voice, and be able to follow his leading. Let's not be quick to dismiss wild and unconventional solutions. It just may be him. In fact, my hope is that you will begin to not only WATCH for these things but begin to desire and pray for these type of occurrences. It's just Jesus, and these are HIS ways.

HEARTCRY: Heavenly father, take me deeper into the revelation of Jesus Christ. Help me not be limited by my past experiences or my narrow earthly thinking, but open my eyes and my ears and my mind to discern your Ways. Your ways are higher, bigger, greater than my ways and my understanding. I want to know you and have the audacity to pray like Moses and Joshua. From this point forth, I want to acknowledge and live like I believe that you can do more than I can ask, think or imagine. Help me to hear the voice of your spirit to know your super natural solutions, your unconventional ways of blessing, and your wild fight tactics.

PART 2

UNIQUE YOU

There is No Place for. Comparison

ndividuality is God's specialty. We are all
individuals. We are all created to have our
own unique journey with the Lord. Your DNA
and fingerprints testify of your individuality. If
we truly are individuals, uniquely fashioned, with
our own personality, will and destiny, then why
do we so often compare ourselves to others? The
feeling of inferiority, isn't relevant because YOU
are created to be YOU. Of course, we all get
inspired by others around us, and I think that's a
good thing. We can look to, and admire, other
brothers and sisters who are living in a level of suc-
cess and victory we don't have, and draw from
them. In fact, we are meant to surround ourselves
with a community, a body of believers, for support and strength. Where we get into trouble

is when we begin to feel sad, down, or inferior because we're not like someone else. That's when the voice of the enemy begins to work. We begin to think things like - I wish I could be that way, or – I'll never be like that. We begin to condemn ourselves to failure or complacency, and it's not based on the truth of God's word, but on our feelings and emotions. In order to follow Jesus, we have to look at Jesus. We have to continue looking at him, because the Bible says as we see him, or "behold" him, we become like him. If we are constantly looking to friends, family, or to other people and things to define us then we lose sight of Jesus. When we lose sight of Jesus, then we lose sight of ourselves in Christ. God wants you to be you.

You Have to Know God for Yourself

You can't borrow someone else's walk with God. You cannot delegate fellowship with the Lord to someone else. It's between you and him. You have to know him for yourself. God has anointed you and called you, not to be like your pastor or like your parents or like your favorite preacher, youth leader or small group friend. He has called you to be loved by him and to fulfill those things he has designed you for. You get to walk with him and build your own relationship with him. God often emphasizes himself as FATHER. YOUR HEAVENLY FATHER. Regardless of how your relationship was with your earthly father, THIS father loves you dearly. He is desiring a real relationship with you. When Jesus prayed, in John 17, he said that eternal life IS TO KNOW God the father and his son Jesus Christ. He first appointed his disci-

He has called you to fulfill those things he has designed you for.

ples to BE with him. It is imperative for each of us to come into a real one-on-one relationship with the Lord for ourselves. It's in those personal exchanges that he strengthens our innermost being and whispers his love for us. It's in those precious moments of intimacy that he often speaks his life-giving words that bear much fruit in our lives.

Only You Can Do What He Designed You for

Many of us suspect that we are created for awe-some things. We have that feeling deep down that we want our lives to be exciting, have impact, and make a difference. I believe that's from the Lord! I believe that's what he had in mind when he created us. But why is it that so many of us are struggling to find our place or end up in jobs we dislike? Or dislike the person we become? Why are so many people just living for the weekend? Why is it that college students change their major so many times?

When we find Jesus we find everything we need for life and godliness.

Let me give you a visual metaphor to keep with you as a reminder.

Take out your keys and look at each individual key. Every key is made differently; every key is made unique; and every key was made to unlock something. Now this is a beautiful picture; a divine metaphor. Just like those keys, every person is created differently; every person is created unique; and every person is created to unlock something here on the earth. But the only way to know what you were created to unlock here on the earth, is for you to connect with the master locksmith, who is Jesus Christ himself. The one who made the keys knows what each one is for. When we find Jesus we find everything we need for life and godliness. In him our very purpose becomes clear. The reason for our gifts and talents, likes and dislikes, becomes evident. Only IN HIM do we find OUR PURPOSE.

This is my personal story: I loved to illustrate from a young age. In fact, I started illustrating comic books in junior high. I was always drawing and painting something. I went to college for design & sound engineering but never finished either degree. I worked at dif-

What do my gifts look like through the eyes of love, service and humility?

ferent agencies doing marketing & graphic design for about six years. I wasn't sure exactly what I wanted to do creatively, but I was really drawn to street art and unique creative expressions. But in my 20's everything dramatically changed. I had an encounter with Jesus and was born again. So much in my life got turned upside down as his grace and beauty transformed me so profoundly from the inside out. The Holy Spirit began to teach me in a different way. Instead of designing posters for parties and nightclubs, I started designing testimony flyers. Instead of getting high and drunk and going to clubs, we started having rave parties, sober and unto the Lord. We began to host poetry nights, break dance competitions, and a gospel centered chill lounge. We began running a coffeehouse in downtown Orlando, Florida called "The Porch". This developed into more and more creative outreaches and ways to share the love of Jesus. I have now been around the world, to about 40 different countries, seeing the Lord do amazing and unbelievable things; and it still continues to develop.

I never could have known the plan of God for my life – I never would have dreamed such an outcome! Now I ask myself, what do my gifts look like through the eyes of love, service and humility – through the eyes and heart of Christ? What do my talents look like when partnering with God? What are his ideas, not my ideas? How can I use every talent and tool for the reconciliation and salvation of my generation? I have taken my talents and placed them into his loving hands. Since I've done that, the understanding and revelation of my life

and gifts have become so much richer, so much deeper and rewarding as I co-labor with him.

I've shared this message in many different places with many different types of people. I've heard some really cool testimonies from people who simply realized their importance in the kingdom and honestly and openly

How can I use every talent and tool for the reconciliation and salvation of my generation?

submitted their gifts and talents to the Lordship of Jesus Christ.

I met two girls from Houston, Texas at the IAM gathering in New York City a few years ago. They were both performing arts majors in college. They wanted to serve the Lord with their talents and prayed about what to do. They explained to me the strategy that the Holy Spirit gave them -- they started hosting creative performance nights. They gathered in a field, on a property close to where they lived, around a bonfire. They invited students who were singers, songwriters, actors, dancers and performers to gather around the comfort of a roaring fire to share whimsical monologues, thoughtful performances, songs, jokes and poetry. They, themselves, began reenacting biblical narratives through various creative performances. Week

after week they created an opportunity to have discussions around these biblical performances.

One time, after speaking at a missionary conference, a young lady came to me and told me she now knew exactly what she was going to do for the Lord. She walked away super excited! Immediately afterwards, she scoped out a neighborhood that needed the life of the Gospel, and began gathering children once a week, on Saturday, to teach them the Bible and give them a snack. The neighborhood was a violent, drug ridden, gang-run area that really needed the power and love of Jesus. She and a friend

We are created individually, on purpose, by the Lord, for his pleasure.

were faithful to minister week after week to the children as their group continued to grow. Soon they were given permission to use a community space. Parents of the children began to get involved, and through a series of events, a year later, we helped them to throw a mini festival in that area. Immediately following the festival, they acquired a space and planted a brand new church with a full-time pastor. We continue partnering with that church to see it grow and bring influence to that entire neighborhood. They just recently shared with me the vision to build a cafe and 5 story training center in that neighborhood. All this happened because this young lady partnered her compassion for children and families with the agenda and plan of God, and stepped out, by faith, to see her city changed.

Another young man I met who was a psychologist explained his journey to me like this: One day he spoke to the Lord saying, "I don't have any gifts or talents, I'm just a psychologist who works with students and addicts." The Lord told him to start two ministries; an afterschool class about purpose and identity in high schools, and spiritual counseling in rehabilitation centers. He offered a five-week spiritual counseling course within a secular rehabilitation foundation. Out of

You are the potter; we are all the work of your hand. - Isaiah 64:8

100 men and women he had 90 sign up for it. And after five weeks he was baptizing 35 of them! We took a team to preach, teach and give testimony at a new rehab he was starting. What a simple way to use a talent to build the kingdom.

God is the potter, we are the clay. We are all truly unique in who we are; and we are created individually, on purpose, by the Lord, for his pleasure. However, we are all called to the same cause. We are all called to be his witnesses, (Acts 1:8), and we are all called to be reconcilers, (2 Corinthians 5:18).

But, we all do it in different ways. There is only one cause, but there are as many methods as there are people. Just like your physical body depends on the UNLIKENESS of each individual part to function, so the body of Christ depends on the UNIQUENESS of its people to fulfill the will of God on the earth.

Every gift you have is a potential weapon of warfare in the hands of the Lord. If he has equipped you with talents, do not take them lightly or limit them to just a hobby. Your gifts are not for personal gain only. They are part of the plan and the cause, to advance the Kingdom.

God Calls and Equips

Jesus turned to his disciples one day, and uttered these frightening words, "If you want to be my disciple you must take up your cross, deny yourself, and follow after me." (Matthew 16) But he also added these words to the fisherman: "Follow me and I will make you fishers of men." You see, as you follow Jesus you may have noticed that he is always prompting you to spread his love and share the good news of the Kingdom.

Whether or not you feel excited about this, or equipped to do it, it is the calling of every believer and the Lord will do it in your life. As long as we are following after Jesus, with our eyes fixed on him, we can be sure HE WILL make us fishers of men. HE will lead and guide us, HE is the one that will MAKE US into a fisher of men. Our part is just to FOLLOW. Just as we fully trust in the Lord for our salvation, we continue in the faith and fully trust him for the empowerment to be a faithful, loving, and bold witness of Jesus Christ. The good news is that he gives you the power to be a bold witness. God continually calls us to do the impos-

The good news is that he gives you the power to be a bold witness.

sible, and then gives us the ability to make it possible. Acts 1:8 says, "You will receive power when the Holy Spirit comes upon you and you will be my witnesses." It is the Holy Spirit of God who gives us the power to be effective witnesses. Don't confuse it. We are not all called to be evangelists, but we are all called to be his witnesses.

The Weak and Foolish

You may not consider yourself to be a very bold witness for the Lord, but this is his goal for you. I've tried to hide behind some of my own objections in the past but I found that the scripture exposes every excuse that I had. 1 Corinthians 1:26-29 states, "Not many of you were wise according to worldly standards, not many were powerful, not many were of noble birth; but, God chose what is foolish in the world to shame the wise, God chose what is weak in the world to shame the strong; God chose what is low and despised in the world, even things that are not, to bring to nothing things that are, so that no human being might boast in the presence of God." I found out that God specializes in using the weak and the foolish in this world. At Evoke we joke around saying that we are the anointed fools, the court jesters of the Kingdom. A lot of people, especially artists and creatives, feel insecure or inferior at times. But God is not challenged by our weaknesses, weird hang-ups, strange tendencies, fears or phobias. He came for the sick, the weak, the bound, the chained, the brokenhearted, the blind and the dead so that he might give them life!

Many people hesitate to step into the calling of God for their lives because they feel unequipped for the position. Moses objected to the Lord saying that he couldn't speak on God's behalf. King David wasn't even called to be a part of the lineup with his brothers when the prophet came. As Jesus walked through the towns, he seemed to pick his disciples at random. He didn't look for the most educated scholars and wise men of the day. He chose ordinary people. And with heaven's eyes he could see the golden potential inside each one of them. The Lord still raises up his people today. I like how Dr. Michael Brown explains God's call on his life. I heard him say something like this, "God wanted to raise up a man to bring a message of repentance, revival, reformation, and cultural revolution, so he looked down from heaven and saw a young heroin addict huffing gasoline from a truck and said, 'That's the one I will use!'"

He's inviting you deeper into his world; to see as he sees; to give you the mind of Christ that you can think like he thinks.

The Lord sees different than we see. He's inviting you deeper into his world; to see as he sees; to give you the mind of Christ that you can think like he thinks. No matter what your past is. No matter what your current status is. No matter what your gifts and talents are. The eyes of the Lord are on you. His heart beats for you. He is inviting you deeper into a love relationship like nothing else. Let him show you HIS plan and PURPOSE for your life. The Lord's ways are so much higher than our ways. We really need to see ourselves the way HE sees us. Let him expand your vision of him today. Let him expand your vision of who YOU are IN CHRIST today. "No eye has seen, nor ear heard, nor the heart of man imagined, what God has prepared for those who love him" 1 Corinthians 2:9

HEARTCRY: Heavenly Father, help me to surrender fully to you. That I would deny myself, take up my cross, and follow hard after you, that you could make me a fisher of men. I give you permission to fill the deepest parts of my being with your Holy Spirit. Make me the person you intended for me to be. You are the potter, and I submit as the Clay to the calling, the shaping, the character building work of your spirit.

PART 3

WORKING WITH GOD

Thinking
Inside the Box

We throw around a common phrase all the time: "THINK OUTSIDE OF THE BOX". It's most commonly used when trying to encourage someone to be creative or think differently—as if all COMMON ideas are within the box of NORMAL thinking, and UNCOMMON, or new creative ideas, are outside that box. I understand that reasoning, but I want to propose a different concept: the idea of THINKING INSIDE THE BOX. We can use the box to propel us forward and to be more focused and precise with our ideas, our time, our money without being any less creative. The box, if seen correctly, can have a great purpose.

The Straight Edges

My kids love to do puzzles; actually, I like them too. But my kids do them differently from me. I was taught to always do the outside edge first. We called it the "straight edge" or the "box". But, my kids like to jump in and start wherever they want. They begin with the tiger face or the train or the balloon—the fun pieces. And they just start putting it together. They get real excited to show me the progress they made in their own little section. The problem with this approach is that although they get a few pieces in place, each kid has a section par-

We must have a context into which everything we do, experience, and work toward, fits into.

tially finished without any context as to how they all fit together. Sometimes it doesn't even look like the same puzzle. But if you do the straight edge first and complete the outer edges or the BOX, it begins to give you a context into which every-thing else fits together to form the whole image.

I believe that in order for us to have a focused, holistic view of Christianity and understand its full context we must recognize the BOX that the Lord has given us. We must have a context into which everything we do, experience, and work toward, fits into. What is the framework or purpose to all this? What is God after? What is Jesus doing?

When we recognize that the BOX of our christianity is simply to know God and make him known, we can begin to move forward. 2 Corinthians 5 gives clarity to the box, "All this is from God, who through Christ reconciled us to himself and gave us the ministry of reconciliation; that is, in Christ, God was reconciling the world to himself, not counting their trespasses against them, and entrusting to us the message of reconciliation. Therefore, we are ambassadors for Christ, God making his appeal through us." When we understand that our career, our business, our family, our

We must recognize the box that the Lord has given us.

ministry, our church activity and our very lives, should fit into the BOX of this GREAT COMMISSION, and we take our places as AMBASSADORS, we have context for every facet of our lives.

In order for us to see God clearly and be effective at working together with the Lord, we need to know what the big picture IS. We have to know God's agenda—God's purpose. To co-labor with him, we first have to believe that God really does have an agenda. If we only see the Lord as some kind of ghost that randomly shows up here and there we will have no way to connect with him. But God does indeed have a purpose and a mission and he is busy accomplishing it. He has revealed it clearly in scripture, the work he has been doing from the beginning. We believe that the original intent of God was to walk together with man in the garden—that

We have to know God's agenda—God's purpose.

God and man would work side-by-side, talking together, and enjoying one another. But since the fall of man, the Lord has been busy with one primary agenda—the reconciliation of fallen man back to himself. He is restoring sinful man to his original identity, his original purpose, his original authority on the earth. This is the work and agenda of God. And this is the work that we have been included in as children of God. This IS the BOX!

Just as a puzzle's straight edge, or BOX gives context to where the pieces go, the Christian BOX of God's agenda gives context to the rest of our Christian life and to the focus of our churches & ministries. More clearly, the agenda of God, the mission statement of Jesus, should frame everything that we say and do and live for. Our personal life, our church life, our creativity, play time, hobbies, families, etc., should be seen within the context of the purpose and will of God.

The Mission Statement of Jesus

In Luke 19:10 Jesus makes this statement, "For the Son of Man came to seek and to save the lost." In fact, he lays out his whole mission statement for us. When Jesus comes on the scene in Luke 4:18 he breaks out the scroll and quotes about himself from Isaiah 61 proclaiming,

"The Spirit of the Lord GOD is upon me, because the Lord has anointed me to proclaim good news to the poor and afflicted; he has sent me to bind up the brokenhearted, to proclaim liberty to captives and freedom to prisoners; to proclaim the favorable year of the Lord and the day of vengeance of our God; to comfort all who mourn, giving them beauty for ashes, and gladness instead of mourning."

The Message translation puts it like this:

God's Spirit is on me; he's chosen me to preach the Message of good news to the poor, heal the heartbroken, sent me to announce freedom to all captives and pardon to prisoners and recovery of sight to the blind. To set the burdened and battered free, to announce, "This is God's year to act!"

Jesus is declaring his mission statement! This is what his life is going to be about. This is why he is here and this is what he is up to. God the father sent him for this purpose. This is God's agenda. God has always been about this and Jesus is continuing with the mission. As you read

Jesus was consumed with proclaiming the Kingdom.

the scriptures, notice how everywhere Jesus went, he was consumed with proclaiming the Kingdom of God and demonstrating it with deep love & compassion, signs, wonders, miracles and a zeal to please and obey God the Father. During the three years he spent in ministry on the earth, he held true to his mission — seeking, saving and restoring all that were lost.

Jesus is still seeking and saving the lost! But now WE do the seeking and HE does the saving. Reinhard Bonnke says, "Jesus saves sinners to save sinners." That's the work we get to participate in! How awesome!

If we don't believe that God wants to crash in on people's lives, here and now today, to save them, heal them and make them whole, then we won't partici-

Jesus is still seeking and saving the lost! But now WE do the seeking and HE does the saving.

pate, believe, move by faith, prioritize our lives, or persist even when the situation looks hopeless.

Your Supreme Commission

Jesus, himself, came to seek and to save that which was lost—save, heal, deliver, set free, release captives, open eyes, destroy bondages, and make all things new. We know this. We read about his amazing works. But then he did something even more miraculous. He commissioned US, his disciples, to do the same. After raising from the dead, just before he leaves earth he turns to his disciples in Mark 16:15-20

And he said to them, "Go into all the world and proclaim the gospel to the whole creation. Whoever believes and is baptized will be saved, but whoever does not believe will be condemned. And these signs will accompany those who believe: in my name they will cast out demons; they will speak in new tongues; they will pick up serpents with their hands; and if they drink any deadly poison, it will not hurt them; they will lay their hands on the sick, and they will recover." So then the Lord Jesus, after he had spoken to them, was taken up into heaven and sat down at the right hand of God. And they went out and preached everywhere, while the Lord worked with them and confirmed the message by accompanying signs.

It is not called the great suggestion, it is God's holy and wonderful great commission.

What an amazing commission we have received! As an artist I have received many commissions, but this is by far the greatest! This is what the purpose of each of our lives should be about. It is

NOT called the GREAT SUGGESTION, it is God's holy and wonderful GREAT COMMISSION.

This means that the mission statement of Jesus now becomes our mission statement. God's agenda is now our agenda.

Do this exercise so it becomes real. Plug in your name and read it aloud. My name would read like this: Scott, go into all the world and preach the gospel to all creation.

I believe that we will get the attention of the Lord when we determine to prioritize the seeking-out of God's lost ones. What I mean is that we begin to enter into real partnering and co-laboring with God doing the most holy eternal work on earth. It's then we see all of Heaven's provisions flow: the supernatural power & love of God, his equipping in us to be bold, exercise faith, hear words of knowledge and experience the power of the Holy Spirit working in us and through us.

Holy Spirit Power

If you have the Holy Spirit, then you are his witness. You are in the club. Matthew 10:7-8 is for you. "As you go, preach this message: The Kingdom of Heaven is near." As you go where? As you go to Wal-Mart, the gas station, or the grocery store, as you go to work, school or visiting friends. Do what? Say, "the Kingdom is near." "Heal the sick, raise the dead, cleanse those who have leprosy, drive out

If you have the Holy Spirit, then you are his witness.

demons. Freely you have received, freely give." Even if you do not want to go to Asia or Africa and be a foreign missionary, when you go to Wal-Mart, you get to proclaim the Kingdom and heal the sick. I thank the Lord for believers that took his work seriously. If not for them I would still be lost.

My Testimony, God's Agenda

I was an atheist until my twenties. I didn't want God, wasn't raised with God, and I could care less. I thought christianity was a crutch for the weak and for people who were afraid to die and needed a fairy tale to calm their fears. But, God had a plan for my life. I had my own agenda, but he also had an agenda. I spent years doing my own thing, running my own life. My decisions lead me to a lifestyle of partying, clubbing, dancing, heavy drinking, and drug use until I lost control of my life. I was free to live my life, but like so many others I was using my freedom to destroy myself. It took the bold witness of so many believers to challenge me to call out to Jesus before I finally, in a moment of what I saw as weakness, gave God just a sliver of a chance. All alone in my room I said my first real prayer to God. My first prayer was "God, if You are real, show up and do something." I didn't hear anything from God - so I gave up.

But the Lord has an agenda. He came to seek and save that which is lost... and I was definitely lost. There were faithful believers in Orlando, Florida who knew God had an agenda and a plan for everyone. After that prayer, it seemed everywhere I went people were telling me that I needed Jesus in my life and that God was reaching out to me. At the gas station, Taco Bell, and even my mailbox! But I didn't put two and two together. I couldn't see that it was the Lord pursuing me! God placed people all around me who invited me to Bible studies and church gatherings. Eventually, I had an encounter with Jesus Christ. I cried like a baby, I felt his presence, I felt his love, I knew he was there. He answered my prayer and showed up! The next day, this guy came into the gas station where I was

Everywhere I went people were telling me that I needed Jesus in my life.

working and shared his testimony about how he, a former drug dealer and his girlfriend, a former stripper, were saved and delivered by Jesus Christ. He took me to his church the next day and discipled me for one year.

That's what Christianity is all about! People stepping into God's will for their lives and then snatching and pulling others into the will of God for their lives.

What a wonderful privilege to be reconciled to our creator. I am ever so amazed and indebted to the Lord for his wonderful salvation. I am saved, clean, and at peace. I love my family, my life and my savior. To be with him and experience his love and beauty is so magnificent. I wouldn't trade it for the world. But reconciliation didn't end with me and it didn't end with you. There are so many more that need to come in. Therefore, he has reconciled us to himself and then GIVEN US THE MINISTRY OF RECONCILIATION.

You are in Full Time Ministry

2 Corinthians 5:17-20

Therefore, if anyone is in Christ, he is a new creation. The old has passed away; behold, the new has come. All this is from God, who through Christ reconciled us to himself and gave us the ministry of reconciliation; that is, in Christ, God was reconciling the world

You will see God do amazing things with your little life.

to himself, not counting their trespasses against them, and entrusting to us the message of reconciliation. Therefore, we are ambassadors for Christ,

God making his appeal through us. We implore you on behalf of Christ, be reconciled to God.

It's imperative that we take time to reflect on these simple and clear scriptures that put such a high demand on our lives. We cannot overlook them. As we recognize, receive and implement these charges on our lives, we begin to step boldly into our roles as believers; and our lives begin to take on the meaning and clarity that we have been praying for. You will see God do amazing things with your little life, your little strength, your gifts & talents, when you take responsibility for your ministry on the earth.

Ambassadors

The definition of an ambassador is: an authorized messenger or representative of the highest rank, sent on a mission to represent a country or kingdom. We are on mission, sent by our king, to represent his kingdom, his agenda, his mission! Whether you feel like it or not, this is what God says about you and this is the authority he has given to you. God has chosen you. He doesn't choose like we choose. He doesn't think like we think. He doesn't function like we function. He is all together

OTHER than us. His ways are higher. As we walk out this christian journey, we have God's Holy Spirit to lead us, guide us and train us in his ways. The scripture says that the spirit of God alone knows the thoughts of God. Let's draw near to our heavenly Father. Let's learn his ways. As we GO and carry out his mission let's watch for his unusual solutions, listen for his voice in unusual places and walk in obedience to his ways. What he says he will do, he will do.

My prayer is that we become strong in our faith, bold in our creativity and bold in our confession of Jesus Christ until this generation comes to know the Jesus we so dearly adore.

When you know that you are a kingdom ambassador and have been commissioned by the King of all Kings, it will radically affect the way you see your life and the way you see all of your talents and interests. We are on assignment from the Lord and have been given the ministry of reconciliation. We are the light of the world, the salt of the earth, and the hope for humanity - this Great Commission supersedes ALL other missions. I believe the Holy Spirit is calling each of us to partner with him in our spheres of influence to see transformation come right where we are. We CAN have great impact!

HEARTCRY PRAYER: Lord, let me boldly love and help me to boldly share the gospel. Give me a steadfast spirit so that I will believe even for those who are the farthest from you to come to faith in Christ. Use me to step into the darkest of lives that your will be done, in them, as it is in heaven. I bring everything I have... every gift, talent & resource... and lay it in the hands of Jesus for the purpose of the reconciliation of my generation! I step by faith into the role you have called me to!

PART 4

ENGAGING CULTURE

We have been given the awesome privilege and great commission to engage and impact our culture with the glorious message of the gospel — the good news of Jesus Christ. We are IN the world, but not OF it! We carry a kingdom within us! Our kingdom is not of this world: we are exiles, sojourners, citizens of another place — Heaven. The Lord Jesus stated that his kingdom was not of this world, but then taught us to pray – YOUR KINGDOM COME, YOUR WILL BE DONE, ON EARTH AS IN HEAVEN! We can pray, and should pray, but then we need to put our prayers into action. We have the unbelievable opportunity to make an eternal impact with our little mortal lives.

No Impact without Contact

If we are really going to have an impact on the people around us we need to have intentional contact with them. That really shouldn't be hard for most of us. We buy food from the same grocery stores as the unchurched. We eat at the same restaurants, work at the same companies, watch the same sports, shop at the same malls, and walk the same streets. Actually all around us every day are opportunities to have kingdom impact. So how do we increase the impact we have on those around us?

As I travelled to a particular part of southeast Asia, we met with a team of Christians who had built a very prestigious university in their country. As they shared the vision of their school they explained to us the desire to graduate educated believers

Actually all around us every day are opportunities to have kingdom impact.

who could, on a professional level, have impact for Christ in the many different spheres of life. You see, their country was dominated by people of another religion, so the goal was to raise up the body of Christ to influence government, business, the arts and all the like.

Afterwards I began thinking. Here, in the United States, we have Christians working in every sphere of society and almost every type of industry you can think of! So why do we have such little impact?

Becoming a Bold Witness

There are a few simple things we can do to start seeing a greater move of God in the lives of those around us.

1. The first is to acknowledge and RECEIVE the CO-mission. The Lord has strategically placed us ALL on assignment, but many of us haven't realized it yet. Or many of us had forgotten that we are on a mission. As we laid out in the previous chapter, *Working with God*, we have to reconcile in our hearts that our purpose on the earth is to co-labor with the Lord on HIS mission. We are not here just for a good career or fun and games, although it IS a blast to serve the Lord. Recognize and receive the charge on your life. By your own admission, Jesus is Lord of your life, you are His ambassadors.

2. Secondly, our hearts need to be stirred. Unless you have completely surrounded yourself in a sterile Christian bubble, you are interacting with unbelievers everyday. These are precious people to the Lord. Sons and daughters who DO NOT know the sweet, loving embrace of

their father. Precious souls that without salvation will NEVER know the father's great love. These are people who make life altering decisions in the dark, without any real moral or spiritual compass. How easy it is to forget the gravity of their situation. How quickly we lose our eternal perspective. We need the Lord to provoke us! We need the bleeding heart of God for these people—a supernatural compassion that moves us into action. In Acts 1:6 we see the Apostle Paul in Athens waiting for Silas & Timothy to join him. But as he walked through the city he was PROVOKED! He couldn't keep his mouth shut and he began to reason with people every-where — the synagogue and in the

The single greatest weekly outreach we have in the church comes every Monday morning.

marketplace with WHOEVER happened to be there it says. Let's pray that the Holy Spirit fans to flame the fervor in our hearts, that we also are provoked to see our generation come to Jesus.

3. The third thing is to recognize WHERE you are. Where has the Lord positioned you? Look around your neighborhood, your school, where you work and where you play. The

scripture tells us that the Lord orders the steps of the righteous. That means that he wants the kingdom of God to come right where you are! The single greatest weekly outreach we have in the church comes every Monday morning. Every Monday morning the body of Christ gets out of bed, filled with the Spirit of God and then heads off in a million different directions. We go to every school in the city, every type of job and workplace, interacting with people of various ethnic groups and religious beliefs. And it's all organized by the Holy Spirit of God! For us to organize such a diverse outreach, would take 12 months of planning, the training up and appointing of various regional directors, with leaders of subgroups and organized prayer teams, etc, etc, not to mention it would take thousands of dollars! Yet the Lord has strategically positioned us, his people, in all these places. Let's recognize the mission fields that the Lord has assigned us to. We are not in the situation like the brothers in South East Asia, trying to populate their country with educated believers. In the USA, we already have God's people posisitoned for impact. Let's stand up and be a witness for Jesus!

4. Fourthly, let's stand up and be BOLD! Bold in love, bold in humility, bold in kindness and

bold with the truth of the gospel. Don't be afraid to stand up and be a witness right where you are. Men and women have lost their lives for this gospel. We can't be afraid to lose just a job over it. I'm not saying to be reckless, we need to be wise. But we also need to be bold. Ask the Holy Spirit what you can do in your sphere of influence. How can you share the love of Jesus and the truth of the gospel? There are as many methods as there are people. Let's renew our enlistment in the army of the Lord and determine to be a soldier in the Kingdom of God.

The Seven Mountains of Culture

The idea of being a missionary within your sphere of cultural influence was made most clear by both Bill Bright, founder of Campus Crusade, and Loren Cunningham, founder of Youth with a Mission. As I understand it, they simultaneously received similar revelations from the Lord about this specific approach. They were the first ones to introduce us to the idea of the 7 *spheres,* or 7 *mountains* of society. The vision was simple: that to transform nations for Jesus Christ, we need to impact the 7 spheres, of society.

The seven spheres they identified were:

1. **Business**
2. **Government**
3. **Media**
4. **Arts & Entertainment**
5. **Education**
6. **Family**
7. **Religion**

The 7 mountains are 7 spheres in society that shape our culture. The thought is that society can be changed or transformed through these 7 spheres.Their assignment was to raise up change agents — people to scale these mountains that would impact nations with the Gospel of Jesus Christ.

The 7 mountains are 7 spheres in society that shape our culture.

Some of us are great at business, others have a passion for education and teaching, while others work in entertainment and media. The commission is to go into all the world and preach the gospel to all creation. All the world! That means the world of SPORTS, the world of GOVERNMENT, the world of FINANCE, the world of ENTERTAINMENT, the world of the ARTS, and more!

What that means is, that no matter what area of expertise, interest, or desire you have, there is Kingdom work to be done. You may have noticed that out of all the spheres, only one of them is called "religion." Building the kingdom of God is not limited to having

No matter what area of expertise, interest, or desire you have, there is Kingdom work to be done.

a role in the church or a ministry. We are ALL Kingdom Builders. In fact, you are specifically designed with gifts, talents, desires, knowledge, and wisdom in specific areas, so that you can carry out the intention of the Lord for your own personal life.

God's goal is not for us all to quit our jobs and join a ministry. God's goal is to make full-time ministers out of every one of us where he has assigned us, while we are accomplishing the work and tasks he has set us out to do. The Hebrew word *avodah* is the root word having the same meaning of "work" and "worship." It's as if God sees our work as worship.

So, if you're an athlete who is training to be a pro-
golfer or an Olympian, you can ask the Holy Spirit,
How can I build the kingdom of God? Or if you're
setting out to be an interior designer, a musician,
restaurant owner, or teacher you can be praying
and asking the Lord how to build the kingdom of
God in your sphere.

Secular and Sacred Forums

We all have unique day-to-day workplace sur-
roundings. Some of us are in cubicles all day,
others are doing delivery or sales calls, others are
doing hard labor or creative work. But whatever
your environment, there is a strategy in the heart
of God to touch each and everyone around us.
We just need to tap into a way that will be effective. Sometimes your platform can be your platform. Other times your platform makes room for
you to create a sacred platform. What I mean
is this: many athletes gain fame and recognition
because of their athletic ability, but when they
are on the soccer field, hockey rink, or

basketball court, they don't have a lot of time, or room, to preach the gospel, give a sermon, or pray for the sick. So the Sports Arena is not really their platform for kingdom building. But, because of their influence and fame, they have a lot of space and opportunity off the field. Their fame in the public platform gives them influence to create sacred platforms for ministry to take place.

However, if you are a REALTOR, and you're showing houses all week long, you have an opportunity to interact with many people on a real personal level. Buying a home is a very personal endeavor. You may have lots of opportunities to have intentional conversations with

In the special times you carve out, you can be intentional to bring the kingdom.

people. So, your public forum is ALSO your sacred forum.

Let's say that you have a small business and your day-to-day activity is running that business. In the way you treat the employees, and the special times you carve out, you can be intentional to bring the kingdom. You might try creating a sacred forum once a week with an optional Bible study for people to share about family matters and give opportunity to pray for one another. You might

have special weekend barbecues or work retreats for families where you can take the time to create a fun and sacred forum where you can share how Christ has impacted you and your family's life.

There's a couple in my church who run a copier business. They heard a message from the pastor about using what God has put in your hand to build the kingdom. Since they're in an area of low income and a large homeless population, they decided to take some action. There was a parking lot next to their building and they decided that God had given them the space and they wanted to use it. They invited some children to come on a Saturday and have some snacks. It went well, so the next Saturday they rented a bouncy house. After that, they started grilling hotdogs and hamburgers. Then parents started coming and the group started to grow. Before they knew it they had a full-on outreach going every Saturday to many families all around the area. Now that outreach has become a church in the second building that they've remodeled right next to their copier business. They didn't set out to be pastors, they just started using what they had to build the kingdom.

> **Create a fun and sacred forum where you can share how Christ has impacted your family's life.**

An artist friend of mine is a talented illustrator. He was doing some amazing drawings, but was frustrated. He asked me the question that I get asked over and over, "How do I use my talents for God?" I invited him out to be a part of a simple park outreach we did. We set up these big wooden doors for him to draw on, next to the percussionists & poets. We spent time in the park having fun, playing music and jamming. Artists were drawing on the doors, poets performing poems, and everyone was having a great time. People stopped and listened and began to talk and open up. It began by them asking him about his artwork. He ended up having quite a few

Sometimes the first step in doing something for the Lord is just to GO and be in the midst of the people.

great conversations, sharing testimonies and praying for a bunch of folks in just a couple hours. That day he learned a very simple principal; the principal of "going." Sometimes the first step in doing something for the Lord is just to GO and be in the midst of the people. When we stand in the marketplace and put ourselves out there, we end up being a light. If you are in Christ, you just shine where you are. I didn't ask him to do a special drawing or a piece of Christian art. In fact I think he did a self-portrait. But the fact that he was in a public place using his gift, was enough to spark some discussions that gave him an opportunity to be bold, have intentional conversations, and be a witness.

We cannot have impact without contact, and if we have contact we can't help but to make an impact. There are SO MANY different, creative & effective ways to engage and interact within our communities. The Lord has given us all various talents, gifts, interests and compassions to cover ALL spheres of culture. I think we can all resonate with the vision of the 7 Spheres.

CS Lewis made an interesting statement about culture: He said that our culture has not become materialistic because of films, books and art about materialism; but because of the production of films, books and art about everything else from a materialistic worldview. We don't need more films, books and art about the Bible, but more films, books and art about everything else from a biblical worldview.

We cannot have impact without contact, and if we have contact we can't help but to make an impact.

Well if this is true, that God wants to send missionaries into every sphere, then we need to take notice. What we are saying here is that the specific make up or bent that draws us towards business, sports, government, the arts or media is not just a random desire, but a strategic plan by the Lord himself to impact and transform society. That means you are not just a business owner, not just a construction worker, not just a web designer, not just a photographer, or financial guy or girl, you are a missionary!

Although there are so many brilliant stories out there, I have collected just a few examples that have shaped my thinking over the years.

Media

Need him is a ministry with the mission to intentionally present the Gospel of Jesus Christ to all people, using all forms of media. In 2008 they released a series of 10 videos, 1 minute long, based on the 10 commandments. The videos were a real fresh animated / real life series called Unreal. Each video starting with the phrase, "Today, I am Unreal". They ran these spots for 3 weeks on MTV and during that time received almost 10,000 phone calls of people asking questions and wanting prayer.

Evoke Ministries created a campaign called My God Encounter. It was a gritty campaign about real people's testimonies in 3 words. We produced thousands of flyers, posters, magazine ads, videos, even a theatre commercial and bus stop ad. We focused on putting flyers and posters all over the University of Central Florida campus, a school of almost 50,000 students. A giant advertisement was placed in the main bus shelter on campus. We even created a 10 second video that ran hundreds of times before the showing of every movie at the nearby movie theater next to the campus. It generated quite a lot of talk & controversy.

A producer for a raunchy talk show called the Jerry Springer show, gave her heart to Jesus and began to consider what she could do for Jesus. She was about to quit when she had an idea. She had a friend working at a faith-based crisis center, which was really a prayer center. She pitched the idea to her boss about having the phone number to the crisis center displayed during the show to provide free counseling, since so many people watching were in desperate situations. Well, they received thousands of calls and many of them gave their lives to Jesus.

Business

As a business owner, you need to get away from the bottom-line mentality, meeting critical deadlines, submitting to policies and politics, and step into the vision of God for your business. Maybe it's just a few small changes, but the biggest change is to know your purpose and perspective; to realize that you run a business to bring the kingdom to the city. That small perspective change can send you on a wild adventure into the miraculous, more than you've ever known in your business. A ship that alters its course, by just one degree, will change its destination by hundreds of miles.

You cannot serve both God and money. Our priority determines our course and measures our progress. What does it look like to bring Kingdom into our businesses? You are an ambassador at your workplace.

Feeding Children Everywhere is a social charity that empowers and mobilizes people to assemble healthy meals for hungry children. They are taking a kingdom concern, which is a real social problem, and making it business relatable. Bringing unchurched people into a kingdom work and having them pay for it. They decided to tackle the horrible curse of poverty on the earth, specifically lack of food. The meal-packaging events offer a way for companies to motivate and involve employees in company-wide activities and help instill a sense of giving into corporate cultures. I participated in a 3-day event in downtown Tampa,

Florida where the goal was to pack 3 million meals to be distributed to schools in south Florida. The company sponsoring the event was JPMorgan Chase Bank. FCE set up huge tents and long assembly lines to pack food in the heart of downtown Tampa. It was an amazing, energetic, fun atmosphere. What I appreciated the most was the praise & worship & prayer that went on during the event and the testimonies that came forth. This wasn't just about the food, this was a faith-filled event for the glory of God. Goodwill opens the door for the good news.

Goodwill opens the door for the good news

Dave Ramsey is a voice for financial freedom that is heard by millions on a weekly basis around the USA and beyond. Dave formed the Lampo group which provides biblically based, common-sense education and empowerment for the purpose of giving HOPE to everyone in every walk of life. His company has created a program called Financial Peace University that is facilitated by thousands of churches every year. Not only does it help people to get straight with their finances and become debt-free, it is driving hundreds of people outside of the church to come in and receive quality teaching and discipleship from a local church. When done correctly, this is an amazing way for people to begin discipleship before even becoming believers!

Chick-fil-A is a quality fast-food restaurant founded by Truett Cathy, a devout believer and follower of Jesus Christ. Chick-il-A stores inside shopping mall kiosks are closed every Sunday. However, it's reported that Chick-fil-A makes more money per store in 6 days than McDonald's does in 7 days. Truett Cathy of Chick-fil-A knows why he

We cannot compartmentalize our faith and our service to God.

has a business -- for the glory of God, primarily. One winter during a horrendous snow storm, displaced people were trapped on a highway in Alabama for hours. The employees of a nearby Chick-fil-A took hundreds of hot sandwiches right to the highway and walked car-to-car, handing out hot food and drinks to everyone they could – free! When interviewed and asked why they did that, the response was simple and clear. The priority of Chick-fil-A is to love people and take care of them, not just to make a profit. That is a KINGDOM business!

A company can have goals; maybe increase of sales by 10 percent this year, or the franchising of three new stores, but they must always have a bottom line that is Kingdom. And the Lord's bottom line is always this: to love the Lord God with all your heart, soul, mind and strength, and love your neighbor as yourself - preaching this gospel and making committed disciples in all the earth.

We cannot compartmentalize our faith and our service to God. Our very lives are an offering, and that includes our money, time, businesses, and talents. Everything that we are, and have access to, are his alone.

You have been created to fulfill your purpose in Christ. Only you can fulfill it. God is looking to you to bring the kingdom. He chose you, and you are the best he has, and he's good with that.

YOU ARE GOD's SECRET WEAPON ON THE EARTH! Your own DNA, your own uniqueness, is necessary for the body to thrive in all fullness.

The Holy Spirit is Our Method

Even though we are always seeking new ways to share the gospel, we don't rely on methods. The

power is not in the method. God anoints men and women not methods. We don't just put a formula into place; we go with a burning heart, a burning message to speak from his burning love. Methods are a means to an end. Acts 1:8 reads *You will receive power when the Holy Spirit comes on you and you will be my witnesses to the ends of the earth!* It is the power and passion of the Holy Spirit that gives us the right motive, the supernatural compassion, the strength and boldness we need for the task he has called us to. Jesus is calling us to the impossible and then making it possible by the power of the Holy Spirit. We may not all be evangelists but we are ALL HIS WITNESSES!

HEARTCRY: Lord What does it look like in my life to influence and bring the kingdom where I am right now with the influences I have in my sphere?

PART 5

GOD CALLS ARTISTS

n this last section I want to speak about the role and calling of the creative believer. God calls artists and creatives of all types. When I say "calls", I mean he singles out and commissions them to a specific task in the kingdom. Many of us feel like there is a bigger purpose to our talent, but we have trouble stepping into it. We know that we can—and should—be using our talents for the Lord but don't always know how to go about it. Not only are so many creative people unsure about it, but, many pastors and leaders have no idea what that looks like either. Because of that, creatives have been completely neglected in the discipleship of their gifts and talents.

Let's take a look at the clearest section of Scripture that we have on this topic.

Exodus 31:1 – Bezalel

Now the Lord spoke to Moses, saying, "See, I have called by name Bezalel, the son of Uri, the son of Hur, of the tribe of Judah. "I have filled him with the Spirit of God in wisdom, in understanding, in knowledge, with ability and intelligence in all kinds of craftsmanship, to make artistic designs for work in gold, in silver, and in bronze, and in the cutting of stones for settings, and in the carving of wood, that he may work in all kinds of craftsmanship. And behold, I have appointed with him Aholiab son of Ahisamach, of the tribe of Dan; and to all who are wise-hearted I have given wisdom and ability to make all that I have commanded you.

That is good!!! You should memorize that! Eat it, drink it, hold onto it and never let it go! This is God's calling, endorsement, and love for artists and creatives. Let's look into this some more.

In his book "Art For God's Sake", Philip Graham Ryken points out that these verses provide at least 4 principals for a Christian theology of the arts:

The artist's call and gift come from God.
God is into all kinds of art.
God maintains high standards.
Art is for the glory of God.

Artists are Essential

Consider this: God specifically chose Moses and Aaron. He came to Moses, called him out of the desert, and gave him a task—to deliver his people from the hands of Pharaoh in Egypt. God was with him. We all know about Moses. He is one of those Bible superheroes doing awesome things for God. BUT, Moses could NOT fulfill all that God called him to without the partnership of artists. Come on! That's for you! Creative guy! Creative girl! Moses needed artists to fulfill God's calling. That is the value of the calling of the Artists.

Moses could NOT fulfill all that God called him to without the partnership of artists.

Just as the Lord called out Moses, he also specifically chose, and called out by NAME, these craftsmen and artists for his service. See, we tend to value some positions over another. We might

Moses needed artists to fulfill God's calling.

elevate pastors or preachers because of their charismatic personality or leadership ability. And it's good that we honor our pastors and leaders, but we are ALL one body. You too have a specific role in the body of Christ and the body of believers in which you live life.

If the Lord calls you to be an artist or creative of some type, then do not resist it. Do not think it is of lesser value or just a luxury or option. The call

of Bezalel and the creative team the Lord put together was just as necessary and important as Moses & Aaron. Let this portion of Scripture give you the validation you need. God is giving gifts to men and women because he has intended for them to serve in the kingdom a specific way as we all work together.

Do you hear the voice of the Lord calling you!?!

I pray that you do not to belittle the gift or ability you have been given. And that you would see it as God sees it, and play your part in the body. Step into your place and calling!

It's not just a hobby

Many people see their interest in creative things as a hobby. It's just something to do when they have free time, or want to unwind a little, have fun and enjoy themselves. Sure, inventing, designing, and building things ARE a lot of fun. So is dancing, photography, cooking, singing, writing and drawing. It's all fun and God is good with fun. In fact, he gives all good gifts for our enjoyment. Of course the Lord has given us these wonderful talents and interests to enjoy—he is like that. I'm sure he takes pleasure in seeing us take pleasure in our creativity. But that is not the only purpose, or highest purpose, that they serve. Your creativity is not just a hobby for you to

Your creativity is not just a hobby for you to have fun.

have fun and dabble with a little on the weekends. What if you have been given a gift, a tool, a weapon a voice to speak life & truth to your generation!?

If Jesus is Lord of your life, that means he is Lord over all of your time, talent and resources as well! Here is the problem with seeing your talents as just a hobby.

If you see your talent as a hobby:

- You will only do it on your free time.
- You will spend very little money on it.
- You do it leisurely.
- Purpose and focus will mean very little.

If you see your talent as a calling or a weapon :

- You will prioritize time to do it.
- You will prioritize your finances towards it.

-   You will do it purposefully, prayerfully,
    and by faith.

If you are creating for your own personal pleasure you may be very frugal on how much money
& time you spend on it. But if you are creating
something Kingdom that is life or death, you will
certainly give yourself permission to have the right
equipment, time, and tools for the job.

Also, treating your gifts and talents as a means
for just a fun career is just short-sighted. Matthew
chapter 6 helps us with this kind of mentality:

"No one can serve two masters, for either he
will hate the one and love the other, or he will
be devoted to the one and despise the other.
(Matthew 6:24-33) You cannot serve God
and money.

"Therefore I tell you, do not be anxious about
your life, what you will eat or what you will drink,
nor about your body, what you will put on. Is not
life more than food, and the body more than
clothing? Look at the birds of the air: they neither sow nor reap nor gather into barns, and yet
your heavenly Father feeds them. Are you not
of more value than they? And which of you by
being anxious can add a single hour to his span

of life? And why are you anxious about clothing? Consider the lilies of the field, how they grow: they neither toil nor spin, yet I tell you, even Solomon in all his glory was not arrayed like one of these. But if God so clothes the grass of the field, which today is alive and tomorrow is thrown into the oven, will he not much more clothe you, O you of little faith? Therefore do not be anxious, saying, 'What shall we eat?' or 'What shall we drink?' or 'What shall we wear?' For the Gentiles seek after all these things, and

We can all imagine a career that would be a blast. But, what is the Lord really looking for?

your heavenly Father knows that you need them all. But seek first the kingdom of God and his righteousness, and all these things will be added to you.

I believe that the Lord gives us talents to provide for our needs. I was able to provide for my growing family for years as a designer. It is righteous to take care of your family. But again, your provision is not the Lord's highest purpose in it. He prioritizes his plans, his agenda, and his people.

We see so many young graduates coming out of design school looking for that perfect career in their field—and why not!? Who wouldn't want to spend the rest of their life doing things like:

- creating hit animated movies at Dreamworks
- photographing space
- being on tour as a dancer, singer, actor
- designing clothes or jewelry
- illustrating books

You get the point.

We can all imagine a career that would be a blast. But, what is the Lord really looking for? What does God want to do? Could it be that God's best idea for you is to work at a secular company, creating things that, at best, don't compromise your morals? I'm not bashing secular work, we should be love and light everywhere, in every place we find ourselves. I'm not telling you to quit your job. I'm not trying to bring any condemnation. I'm saying, "Let's dream bigger!" Let's dream with the Lord. Let's put our talents into his hands and ask him what he has in mind.

I believe that God is wanting to bring things to the earth that will rock a generation!

- A film
- A book
- A dance
- A story
- A picture
- A blog
- A design
- An idea
- A concept

Bring something that carries the very power & presence of God to wake a whole generation!

He is calling creatives into a sphere of partnership with him that will cause an explosion of ideas and information to flood the earth with his glory!

Let's commit to seek first the kingdom of heaven and see where that takes us. Let's decide today that the talents we have could possibly bring great change in our day to our generation. Let's take responsibility and get serious about the plan of God. That is the ideal way to prioritize kingdom creativity in your heart.

Start thanking the Lord for His desire to create. He has given you these gifts. Don't see it as just a hobby or a fun thing that you do. Open your eyes

to see what God has in mind and begin using your talents for greater kingdom purposes!

Creativity is a Spiritual Work

You see, creating is actually a very Spiritual work. The Scripture points out, in Exodus 31, that Bezalel was filled with the Spirit of God, in wisdom, in understanding, in knowledge, and in all manner of workmanship. This is actually the first biblical mention of someone being FILLED with the spirit. Up until then, the Bible says the Spirit 'came upon' them. God supernaturally enabled Bezalel to do the work of building the Tabernacle. God saw this work as just as spiritual, and just as dependent on the Holy Spirit's power, as the work Moses and Aaron did. Wow! Creativity is spiritual work! So the Lord saw it was necessary to fill a man with the Holy Spirit so he could create things. We NEED the Holy Spirit. We NEED to learn to partner with him in our work. Maybe it's kind of foreign to you to invite the Lord into your creativity. If you are a singer, dancer, photographer, fashion designer, or videographer you should learn to worship and fellowship with the Lord as you create. We need to develop a real dependency on the Holy Spirit. I've heard new Christians, that we work with, say they can't play music like they used to because they have always played drunk. Or illustrators who can't design as well because they were always high on something. You see, there is a retraining, or a renewing of our hearts and minds, to really learn to create in the presence of God. What used to be a dependency on a substance now needs to be replaced with a dependency on a person—the Holy Spirit of God. The pro-

God is wanting to bring things to the earth that will rock a generation!

cess is real and it's ok to begin learning now if you haven't already begun that journey. We want to be those who, IN FAITH and by the POWER OF THE HOLY SPIRIT, create works unto God that fulfill his purposes.

When you understand that creativity is not only just a mental, imaginative work, but that it's also a partnership and empowerment from the Spirit of God himself, you will begin to experience new depths of productivity and intimacy.

Begin to pray for your creativity, skill, wisdom, and ability that you would be sensitive to the leading of God's Holy Spirit. Retrain yourself to welcome the Holy Spirit into the process and activity of your inspiration and execution.

Art for God's sake

"That they may make all that I have commanded you". (Exodus 31:6)

Bezalel and his team were part of the bigger picture – the body of Christ – the work of God in a people, in a nation. It was for the Lord's purpose. The Lord gave Moses a vision to accomplish a purpose. The Lord called together a team for that purpose, and everyone had a role.

We are all part of a larger body. There is more at stake here than just your own career, calling, or ministry. Each one of us is so uniquely special, valued, and created by the Lord. Each one of us needs to be confidently standing in our given position so that the body functions as a proper unit. The creative believer is desperately needed to serve the purposes of God. A lost and dying world is suffering without the role of the imaginative, creative believer walking in the power of their calling. It's like the body is limping along because we have neglected to stand up, in our place as creative believers.

God's empowerment isn't to be used for our own selfish ends. It's not for us to make OUR NAME KNOWN, but for us to make the NAME OF THE LORD KNOWN.

We all have our dreams and visions for the future. But, I believe that the Lord is looking for those who will dream his dreams; those who will allow his visions into their heart. As hard as it is, it's imperative that we find the strength in prayer to lay all of our creative hopes, dreams, and visions

We cannot just create for creativity's sake, but it must serve the purposes of Christ...

at the foot of the cross of our Lord & Master, and ask him to fill us with his will for our lives.

I can remember clearly a time in my life when I did just that. I had been working as an illustrator & designer for 8 years when my life took a complete turn into short-term missions. I remember that after just a short time of doing mission work that my wife and I knelt in our living room and surrendered our hearts. It went something like this: "Lord I am willing to lay down all things creative. If you are calling us to mission work in Africa, we will do it. We are scared and don't know what that looks like, but we will go if you go with us and give us the strength." We meant it. It was roughly 3 years later when we felt called to begin the creative evangelistic ministry of Evoke. I was prepared to put aside everything creative that I had done for years. In this case, it was his will for me to continue moving forward. After 5 years of missions the Lord wove together my years of creative learning with the years of overt evangelism and power, and he fashioned a unique path for my life.

I'm convinced if we walk with the posture that creativity is for God's sake, and not our sake, then we will find him leading us into some very interesting places by his Spirit.

"They were all filled with the Holy Spirit"—not to work unto themselves, but to recognize the call of God and take their rightful place. We cannot just create for creativity's sake, but it must serve the purposes of Christ, which is seeking and saving those who are lost and making committed disciples.

Let's determine to have a heart that is turned toward God—doing all things as unto the Lord. Submit your dreams, goals and desires to the Lord.

Lay them at the foot of the cross and cry out to him saying, "Not my will but your will be done."

Idols

Artists need to watch out for pride. We are always being praised for our creativity. How often do you hear, "You are so talented!" or "That's amazing! How do you do that?". It feels good to get validated for your work and that someone actually appreciates it! But it can be a real trap for our hearts.

Consider the group of Israelites that Moses was leading. As they were leaving Egypt in Exodus 12:35, Moses told them to ask the Egyptians for silver and gold jewelry. Crazy enough, they gave it to them! It says that the Lord had given them favor in the sight of the Egyptians. What a huge blessing! They came out of bondage and slavery and then received piles of silver and gold! But check out what happens in Exodus 32. Moses was on the mountain talking to God and getting instruction. In the meantime, the people came to Aaron and asked for new gods. Aaron agreed and said, "Bring me the rings of gold from your wives, sons & daughters". He took the gold and made a calf out of it and said, "These are your gods, Israel". Where did a group of wondering slaves get golden jewelry? It must have been what the Lord blessed them with when leaving Egypt. I am sure the Lord had the tabernacle in mind when he gave them the gold, but they squandered it on there own little idols.

Here's the point—Israel took the blessings of God and turned it into an idol! And many times, we as artists and creatives take the blessing of God, (our God-given gifts & talents), and make them into our idols! It becomes all about us; all about creating for our own pleasure, our own gain, or our own notoriety. We do things OUR way.

Sometimes the idol can come from pressure to do it "their way". This is what happened to Aaron. He was a priest, called to lead with Moses, yet he buckled under the pressure to satisfy **We MUST be lovers and pleasers of God alone.** the wants and requests of the people. It happens too many times in our churches. Creatives do the same. You may work in an industry whose trends and moral standards don't thrive off the values of Christ. The pressure to change lyrics as a musician, tweak imagery as an artist, or to dress, design, or speak in order to appease an industry or audience we love and respect, goes against the convictions of the Scripture and Holy Spirit, revealing

the idols that live hidden in our hearts. We have to look beyond our talents and see more than talent, career, a fun time, or a desire to create something new. Reinhard Bonnke says, "I am immune to the criticism of men, because I am immune to the praise of men." This means that if you don't let the praise of men build up your heart, you will not be harmed or affected by their criticisms. We MUST be lovers and pleasers of God alone.

We have been invited into God's divine plan—to co-labor with him for his purposes. With our earthly hands and our gifts and talents, we can help build the Lord's eternal kingdom!

We cannot do art for art's sake, but art for God's sake. It is by his power, for his glory we create!

Releasing Presence

When Moses and all the craftsmen were finished building the tabernacle, the end result was nothing less than spectacular. Exodus 40 records that when everything was put in place, a cloud covered the tent and the glory of the Lord filled the tabernacle! I believe this should be the model for our artistic endeavors and projects—that the glory of the Lord would rest upon it. God is no longer in the temple Holy Place. We are the temples of the Holy Spirit. He dwells in us and upon us.

The aprons of Paul the apostle healed the sick and tormented. (Acts 19:11-12)

The musicians of the praise team of Jehoshaphat defeated the army. (2 Chronicles 20:20-22)

The sculpture of the snake cured poisonous infections. (Numbers 21:7-9)

Our lives and what we create can now carry the very presence of the Lord, bringing healing and restoration to our generation! We have seen artworks, poems and dances heal

The creative believer is desperately needed to serve the purposes of God.

disease, bring deliverance, and reconcile prodigal children. The creative believer is desperately needed to serve the purposes of God. A lost and dying world is suffering without the role of the imaginative, creative believer walking in the power of our calling. It's time that we understood these weapons of warfare that the Lord has equipped us with, and begin to fight the way he made us to fight. A generation depends on it.

Let's determine to create in a way that the Glory of the Lord and the power of the Holy Spirit can move upon all those who come in contact with it.

The Language of Creativity

When I began to work as a graphic designer I went through the process of learning a very important lesson and skill. I learned to completely separate my personal expressions and likings from my professional creative work. When I was doing design work for a bank, I communicated what they wanted me to communicate. It was not a personal expression. Through a logo, color, font, text, or design, a company may convey itself as strong, creative or environmentally friendly. Design communicates through a different language. As generations change, creative people learn to communicate differently. We are translators of, and in, our day. As believers we are translators of a message and of a man and his kingdom. We dare not change the message. It may take different forms or appearances, but the core message must remain true. We can contextualize but never compromise. For God confirms HIS word, not our words. Let's not leave people hanging as to what we are saying through what we create. We have a wonderful message that everyone needs to know. Of course parables and storytelling are wonderful vehicles for gospel truth and give room for people to seek out truth for themselves. We need to be sure that when they do dig deeper the truth is there for them to find.

HEARTCRY: Heavenly Father, raise up a the creative generation for the Kingdom of God! I pray that every creative would recognize the purpose you have placed inside of them. I surrender my gifts and talents to you and your purposes. Help me to see them differently - no longer just a hobby, but a divine tool. Teach me to create on your behalf, for your glory.

CONCLUSION

The days are dark but we are in a time of amazing moves of God, ready for the greatest harvest ever seen. The sons and daughters of God are being called into battle and thrust out as laborers into the fields of the earth. We are salt and light in an ever increasing wasteland, baptized and equipped with the power, love and boldness of God's precious Holy Spirit and armed with tools and talents – gifts given from the Father of Heavenly lights.

If you are breathing then you are a part of the Lord's last days army. I saw a vision once. It was the army of God. They were marching together in unison. They were in uniform, nicely synchronized as they walked together, just like you would expect the military to be. But as that group passed me I saw another group coming. They were NOT in typical uniform. They were in jeans, shorts, colored pants with sneakers, flip flops, dress shoes. In their hands they had phones, tablets, paintbrushes, pencils and more. Others had cameras and gear hanging off their shoulders, some riding skateboards and BMX bikes, others holding surfboards, microphones and all kinds of stuff. I knew they were also the army of God. And although they didn't walk or talk in a uniform fashion there was still a real unity among them, and still a sub-mission to the overall mission.

God's end-time military looks like YOU and looks like ME! Very ordinary people doing extraordinary things with the skills, talents and characteristics that the Lord has given us. Stop wondering if the Lord is calling you and know that you have been invited to walk close and to work together with him. The Lord has appointed you to be with him and to go and share the gospel. (Mark 3:14).

My hope is that this book has in someway expanded your understanding and opened your mind to the ways of God and that you would no longer overlook how special, how unique, how individual the Lord has made you. I hope it has taken away some of the mystery of serving God, and you would begin to hear the Holy Spirit leading and guiding you in every day life with every day things.

Stand up, take your place, walk the grace of God, go in the power & love of the spirit, take what's in your hand and become a sign and a wonder to this generation. Let the light and love of the gospel of Jesus Christ be proclaimed, demon-strated, and lived out in you and through you as you enjoy your journey with Him.

The Author

Scott Howe has journeyed from Art Student/Atheist to Creative Evangelist. This Canadian born chocolate lover worked in over 35 countries along side evange- list Reinhard Bonnke and the Christ for all Nations team. In 2008 he founded EVOKE CONCEPTS, a creative evangelistic ministry focused on sharing the Gospel through creative mediums and empowering the church to be bold in creativity and confession of Christ.

Evoke. Ministries

Event Outreach:
Evoke hosts many different types of public events to preach Jesus and interact one on one using all kinds of creative approaches.

Mobilizing the Church:
Evoke works with churches of many denominations offering training, teaching, preaching & activation via presentations, classroom training, street activation and outreach. Our goal is to come alongside

churches and groups who desire to be more active and effective in witnessing and sharing their faith in the love, power & creativity of the Holy Spirit.

Compelling Creatives:
The creative believer is desperately needed to serve the purposes of God in our generation. One of the aims of Evoke is to validate & empower the imaginative, creative believer to step into their calling and walk in the power of the gospel.

Resources

Books & Workshop
For information on ordering books, hosting a Kingdom Creativity workshop at your church or ministry, getting a downloadable workbook, and more!
kingdomcreativitybook.com

Evoke Website
Get more information about Evoke, join our mailing list and find other creative resources, events, videos and updates!
evokeministries.org

Online Store
Shop for original art and gifts created by our artists and help support the mission work of Evoke Ministries.
evokestudioorlando.com

Contact us at:

Evoke Ministries
PO Box 720866
Orlando, FL 32872
scott@evokeministries.org

Notes, thoughts & ideas

Notes, thoughts & ideas

Notes, thoughts & ideas

CPSIA information can be obtained
at www.ICGtesting.com
Printed in the USA
LVOW06s1932270617

539564LV00015B/32/P